It's All About Him

AZALEE BELLAMY

I dedicate this book to all my loved ones: family, friends, grandchildren, and great grandchildren. I pray it brings wisdom to all readers; comfort to those in need of comfort and be enlightenment to those in need of knowledge. And last, but not least an introduction to the man Jesus, who is my life, my strength, my all.

SECTION I

I AM THAT I AM
LET LOVE BE THE CHANGE
WHAT THE WORLD NEEDS NOW
LIVE LIFE
WOULD YOU BE GUILTY
FATHER'S PROTECT YOUR CHILDREN
START WITH JESUS

I AM, THAT I AM

I was he, that was, before the foundation of the earth,
I knew your name even before your birth.
Counted the stars that are in the sky,
Know all the answers of when, where, and why

I am that I am
I knew of your conception in your mother's womb,
I called forth a dead man from the tomb.
Performed many miracles and wonders so great,
Never did I sin or make a mistake.
I am that I am

I've given out talents, and gifts without callings,
Great works were accomplished, some to honor and appalling.
I know of the past, the present, and yet to be
Gave Moses a rod that departed the red sea.
I am that I am

In me there is purpose, and great destiny
I'm part of a mighty three-fold trinity
I'm Alpha and Omega, the beginning and end
Was part of creation before it began
I am that I am, know ME!

LET LOVE BE THE CHANGE

There is a shortage, in the world today
Too much hate and no time to pray.
It seems so hard but not so strange,

Let's let love be the change
Too much crime, and murders going on,
No safety on our streets or even in our home
A hard pill to swallow, but not so strange,

It's time to let love be the change
No news is good news, anymore so it seems
It's racial and bias by all that it deems
A time to be prayerful, but not so strange

But time to let love be the change
What the world needs now is not more hate,
Or judges in courtrooms to determine your fate.
Not policemen in uniforms, misusing their power
Or mobs demonstrating, saying this is our hour.

It seems very frightening, but not so strange
Let's get it together, and let love be the change.

WHAT THE WORLD NEEDS NOW

Jesus is the answer for the world today
To a wicked generation, now gone astray.
He's a problem solver and a mind fixer,
A soothing salve and an awesome elixir.

He can brighten your day when you're feeling down,
Cast a big smile out over a frown.
Put joy in your heart, take away your sorrow
Give abundant hope to face your tomorrow.

He's waiting and knocking at the door of your heart,
Allow him in and don't let him depart
He'll alleviate all the pain that you feel
Trust in him, your body he will heal.

Jesus is the name above all others,
Treat you better than your sister or brother
Be that lawyer in a huge courtroom
When facing your life to a prison of doom.

He'll save your soul from hell and shame,
Just by calling upon his holy name.
When you've failed in life doing things your way,
Remember Jesus is the answer for this world today.

LIVE LIFE

As I woke up this morning, I turned on the news
So much chaos and calamity, not much to amuse
Too many killings and murders at all time high
I threw up my hands and ask God why

The bible will tell us that these are the signs,
That the end is near and shorter is the time.
And think it not strange of the trials we face,
But be thankful for all his mercy and grace.

Continue to spread the great gospel of Christ
For in him we are living our very best life.
Don't forsake the people we see on the street
With cardboard signs needing something to eat.

Reach out to the children, that live in a broken home
Believing they're the reason that they are all alone.
Show them love with compassion and hugs along the way,
You'll never know how much you've made their day.

So, we live our lives, one day at a time,
Between love and hate is a very thin line.
And safety is in the arms of Christ
Because now I'm living my very best life.

FATHER'S PROTECT YOUR CHILDREN

Fathers you are called to be the head of the house,
Teach your children, and love your spouse
Guide and lead them to do what's right
Pray for them always when out of your sight.

Show them examples of how to treat their mother,
Trusting in God, and above all others.
Love them with an unconditional love
Not with material things, but gifts from above.

Train them up in life, the lessons they should keep
That whatsoever they sow, they will also reap.
Allow them to learn from the mistakes they make,
No matter the lesson or how long it takes.

Fathers protect your child no matter the cost
Praying over them caring that their souls not lost.
It's a very cruel world their growing up in,
Teach them the difference between righteous and sin.

Giving life lessons along the way,
Show them how to fast and pray.
Be the best dad that you can be,
An awesome roadmap to their destiny.

WOULD YOU BE GUILTY

If loving the lord was a major crime,
How many folks today would be doing time?
Who would be arrested for doing good deeds?
Preaching the gospel and sowing good seeds

If reading the bible was a brutal sin,
And you'd get sentenced from five to ten,
Who would stand and say guilty as charged?
Or would you run and be a criminal at large?

If teaching your children, the right way to go
Was considered by law a grave no- no
Who would stand up and fight for the cause?
Implement Christ to change the laws?

If living for Christ was a total disgrace,
I'd plaster his love all over the place
I'd be a felon sentenced for life,
But so worth it, if I'm living for Christ.

START WITH JESUS

You've got to atone for all the things you've done,
That was not pleasing in the sight of the lord.
And make amends to the people you've wrong
Or you'll never receive the reward.

You must lay aside the sins and weights,
That has kept your life bound down,
Correct and conquer over your mistakes,
Or forever be lost and not found.

You must forgive constant not holding a grudge
Over loved ones and so- called friends
Unforgiveness is like a stain and a smudge
That will lead to a bitter end.

So, in order to live an awesome life
With a renewed mind and clean heart,
Get rid of all malice, envy and strife,
And let Jesus, be where you start.

SECTION II

I PLEDGE TO GOD

GOD'S GOT MY BACK

GOD'S FAVOR

FATHERLY WISDOM

ALAS I'M FREE

HELP ME LORD

NOT ME, BUT ALL ABOUT HIM

I PLEDGE TO GOD

I pledge allegiance to my god
The one who was and yet to be,
Who died and rose to live again,
In him I gain all my liberty.

I trust in him whose blood was shed,
So, my sins would be forgiven,
The cross he carried to Calvary's hill
Is the reason why I am living.

And by his stripes I am healed,
No sickness he cannot cure,
My life I'm placing in his hands,
For my redemption in him is sure.

So, with salvation I am sealed
Till he returns one final day,
I'm waiting and watching, holding to faith
When the rapture will take me away.

I pledge allegiance to my God,
The Lord of Lords and King of Kings
The message of hope he gives to all,
And an eternity in heaven it brings.

GOD'S GOT MY BACK

There were times in my life, that I felt all hope was gone,
Searching here and there, listening to, a profound gospel song.
The music is so soothing it keeps my mind on track,
It's then that I discovered that, God's got my back.

There is chaos all around us, like each- and every day
My mind would just go crazy if I hadn't, took time to pray
But God in all his glory, gives me comfort where I lack,
Never leaving me to doubt, that he's always got my back.

The trials just won't stop coming, they come to make me strong,
My faith in God, will help me continue to hold on.
This journey will be a challenge, with hopes and dreams in- tact,
And I will reach my destiny, because God will have my back.

GOD'S FAVOR

Lord grant me favor in thy sight,
To live for you and do what's right
No matter the test that comes my way,
But seek your face both night and day.

And be not dismayed by what I see
But be steadfast, always true to thee.
To give thee praise along the way,
Honor and repentance when I pray.

Be kind to others that I meet
Avoid confrontation, and always discreet.
Your favor is priceless, a blessed reward
Granted and given, only by our Lord.

O grant me favor lord in this life
Not with materials, vain things or strife.
But give me grace seasoned with love
That only comes from God above.

FATHERLY WISDOM

Fathers teach your children to do what's right,
Show them love each day and night.
Teach them principles and facts of life
Show your sons how to treat a wife.

Be that hero that they look up to
With honesty, trust and respect for you.
Lead by example, as the head of your house,
Even leading alone, if you don't have a spouse.

Teach your girl the type of person to marry,
So, they don't end with extra baggage to carry
The best foundation that you can lay
Is bible knowledge and bible way.

Fathers don't leave your kids to roam,
Too many grow up products of broken homes.
Unruly and lacking no respect to anyone
They are someone's daughters, and they are someone's son.

ALAS I'M FREE

As I look in the mirror at the person I see
The image seems flawed, but it's still me.
Age spots and wrinkles are openly there,
And gray strings are appearing all over my hair.

The image that's staring back at me
Has beauty and aged quite graciously
The lord has forgiven my life complete
I know in my heart alas I'm free

No boundaries or borders holding me back,
The Lord makes up the structure where I lack
I'm believing and trusting his plan for me
That will lead me on to my destiny.

So, when I'm staring at the mirror once more
I'll feel all the goodness that lies in store
And without the Lord, there is no me
But in my soul alas I'm free

HELP ME LORD

Open my eyes Lord, that I may see
All the dangers present, that come to hinder me
Guide me safely along the way,
Be my shelter both night and day.

Protect me now, even when I call
Pick me up when I stumble and fall
Show me the right paths to take,
That I won't make the same mistakes

I want your mercy and your grace,
To help me run this Christian race.
And when I'm tried and challenged too
Take my hand and see me through.

Open my mind and let me know
The path you lead that I should go.
And when down here my race is won
I want the Lord to say, "well done".

NOT ABOUT ME BUT ALL ABOUT HIM

I need to be free, patient and kind
Not letting any problems cloud my mind
Taking in moments, I don't want to miss,
And crossing out things on my bucket list.

I've got to appreciate the life I live
Be willing to sacrifice, and, also to give,
Not take for granted what God has done,
When he sent his one and only son.

I'm living the life he chose for me
Blessed each day to wake and see.
It's quite amazing the way I feel,
No one can tell me that God isn't real.

I give God the praise that I feel inside
Not about lust or even about pride
It's not about me, but all about him,
Taking my life well above the rim

SECTION III

WHEN LIFE DON'T MAKE SENSE
PRIDE DESTROYS
LIFE IS A VAPOR
IF MONEY IS THE ANSWER
DON'T PANIC JUST PRAY
WHAT'S YOUR ISSUE?
LIFE IS PRECIOUS

WHEN LIFE DON'T MAKE SENSE

I attended a funeral of a loved one now gone,
Heard their bio of life, and a favorite song
A death so tragic, the order so immense,
We ask God why, it don't make sense

They were young and vibrant, with friends galore
Who'll be missed by them each day more and more
So, who will now aid in their defense?
When life right now just don't make sense

We cry and we hurt with each passing day
Searching as why it happened this way
We must move forward, avoid the past tense
Because life sometimes just don't make sense.

But God sits high, and he knows all things
That comes in seasons of joy and change
And though we'll never quite recompense
Because life sometimes, just don't make sense.

PRIDE DESTROYS

Pride led by boasting begats much destruction,
And then when finished, promotes your corruption
Life as you know it will never be the same,
Until you finally make a change.

Don't let pride become your friend,
It'll only lead to a bitter end.
You'll come up short and make mistakes,
Because pride is a fixture that Jesus hates.

Don't look down on others, on your way to the top
When you least expect, they'll see you flop
Pride will take you farther, than you ever want to go,
Literally destroy you from your head to your toe.

Don't let pride build up in you,
And take control of all you do.
Follow the Lord that sits on the throne,
With life in him, you can't go wrong.

LIFE IS A VAPOR

It's appointed unto man once to die,
We don't know when, where or why
We need to be ready for that notable day,
When life on earth is dissolved away

For we are as pilgrims passing through
Must give an account of the good we do.
We must live each day and do what's right,
And to be pleasing in God's sight

We must see the need to help each other,
Be there for our sister and brother.
Spread God's love across the world,
To every child boy and girl.

And when our time on earth expires
We've done what only God requires
Your soul will leave that earthly shell,
To go where only our Lord will dwell.

So, when death knocks upon your door,
It's then too late nothing more.
So, live each day, like it's your last,
Your future will be better than your past.

IF MONEY IS THE ANSWER

There are things in life, that money can't buy
What you possess are the lust of the eye
And love isn't love till you give it away,
If truly meant to be, it would always stay.

If health could be bought with a given price,
The rich would all live and the poor would suffice.
And if money could buy a world of peace,
Then all the wars and murders would cease.

If money could buy happiness, souls would be blessed
But reality is this that flesh is a mess.
Unless we accept Jesus to come in our life,
They'll always be conflict, envy and strife.

Money is good and a blessing to have
But don't worship it like the golden calf
For the love of it is the root of all evil,
To make it an idol will surely deceive you.

Jesus is the way the truth and the life,
He'll give you peace and take away strife
And give that everlasting eternal love,
That only comes from God above.

DON'T PANIC JUST PRAY

With all that's happening in the world right now,
And so many questions of why and how
We search for answers in every way
And I say to all don't panic, just pray.

There's so much chaos around the world,
Like searching an oyster to find a big pearl.
Trouble is common we hear of it each day,
But don't you panic now just pray.

We see on the news of such horrible acts
Of murders and suicides and all out attacks.
Of children leaving home and going astray,
Yet listen don't panic just pray

In times like these we need a cure
Where minds are focused, and hearts are pure.
So, when you're speechless and no words to say,
Always remember don't panic just pray.

WHAT'S YOUR ISSUE?

We all have issues, some big some small,
Things we can't handle, too complex to recall.
Attitudes we get when we had a bad day,
Cause nothing that happened, went our way.

The boss made you angry, and the co-workers too,
But you couldn't afford to leave the crew.
You went to the bar when you got off,
Got to your house drunk and slept in the loft.

You have issues with money, because you don't have enough,
Been busy just spending on useless other stuff.
Issue with bills that you didn't pay
Cause you are grown just having your way.

But with issues in life, there is a fix
Began adding the Savior to the mix.
There's no issue too hard, that he can't solve
Whatever the situation that you're involved

So, gather your issues one by one,
Give them over to God's only son
He'll take care of all your problems
No better person than him to solve them.

LIFE IS PRECIOUS

I'm living for this moment, my past I can't forget
Tomorrow is not promised, yesterday I won't regret.
Sometimes we lose our focus, dwelling on the things we lost
You can't undo what's done by any means or cost.

Start living in the present, look forward to each day
Use the gifts that are within you, to guide you on your way.
Don't ever take for granted the time that you are here,
Stop reliving all the tragedies, that happened just last year

Start smiling every morning, have a reason to face the day,
And cherish every moment, before life is vanished away.
Hold on to precious memories, that often make you smile,
They'll keep you moving forward and won't cramp your style.

SECTION IV

GOD'S PURPOSE FOR YOUR LIFE
BEWARE OF THE TEMPTER
BE MINDFUL OF YOURSELF
SINNERS NO EXCUSE!!
JESUS IS AT YOUR DOOR
JUST LISTEN
W.W.J.D.

GOD'S PURPOSE FOR YOUR LIFE

We were all born with a purpose,
That we didn't even know
But life's lessons along the way
Would soon tell us so.

There are paths we travel down,
Through bitterness and strife
It's not what's meant to be,
God's purpose for your life.

Life gives you some direction,
You choose it right or wrong,
Take the bible as your handbook,
It will guide you all along.

Your talents and aspirations,
And gifts that you acquire,
Are all apart of knowing
The purpose of God's desire.

BEWARE OF THE TEMPTER

Beware of old Satan, who comes in many forms
Never to encourage, but always do you harm.
He knows time is short, and his days are very few
Look out for the scammers and con artist too.

His tactics are skillful, so, a word to the wise
Be careful and watchful of his cruel disguise.
To the Seniors don't be fooled when someone calls,
Saying your social security is stolen, etcetera and all.

Hang up your phone, because hackers are real,
Always info and money are things that they steal.
Don't get blind sighted, when a message is sent,
Pretending they're family full of evil contempt.

Money scams are real in this day and time,
Always be careful and keep this in mind.
Satan's job has been to kill, steal, and destroy,
Using thieves, con-artist and imps he employs.

Be prayerful and watchful in all that you do,
And know that your God will watch over you.

BE MINDFUL OF YOURSELF

Be careful when you so often complain,
For you know not what lies ahead
Someone slept on the ground last night,
While you were asleep in your bed.

Be mindful when you say that I,
"Don't know just what to eat"
While your cupboard is full of food and drink,
There's someone hungry, begging on the street.

Be watchful how you often complain,
Saying" what have I to wear"
Your closet may be very over- flowing,
Not one hanger left to spare.

Be careful to whom you entertain,
While looking down on some
And favoring those in gay apparel,
And sneering at the bums.

You never know to whom you meet,
As you travel from day to day,
For some have been God's angels,
That he just sent your way.

"SINNERS NO EXCUSE"

Some people will never read the bible,
Or listen to a sermon on tv
So, I will share the goodness
Of Christ that shines through me.

They won't turn on the radio,
To listen to a gospel song
But best believe they're watching,
To see me when I've done wrong.

Some won't attend the church chapel,
They say it's not their style
It's full of hypocrites and preachers
That greet you with a smile.

But note the day is coming,
When all the world will know
That the bible isn't a fairytale,
And Christianity, isn't a show.

There won't be any excuses,
It's quite plain to see,
I'm enjoying my very best life
With Christ that shines through me.

JESUS IS AT YOUR DOOR

You're in need of help, but say leave me alone,
Spiraling out of control, cause you say that you're grown.
Jesus is knocking so, just let him in,
He can change your situation and renew you again.

Your family is praying for you to get help,
You're stuck in a rut all by yourself.
Jesus is knocking please let him in.
He's the only resource to deliver from sin.

Your problems are mounting, but you can't see,
Blinded by something that can't set you free
You won't accept help from family and friends,
The road you're on leads to a dead end.

Wake up my child before it's too late,
When death and judgement, becomes your fate.
Jesus is knocking, so don't turn him away,
Open your heart to him, please don't delay.

JUST LISTEN

If we take the time to listen, when trials come our way,
And don't be rash in judgement or utter the things we say
If we take the time to listen, when our hearts are filled with sorrow
Then the good that lies within us, will better our every tomorrow.

If we take the time to listen, to our neighbors when they're in need,
Aid the homeless and the widows and bless them with good deeds
If we take the time to listen, when we pray and seek the lord,
Our fears won't overtake us, and peace will be our reward.

So, take the time to listen, hear what God is telling you,
Your life will be much better, and your future will be too.

W.W.J.D. (WHAT WOULD JESUS DO)

Sometimes we say the slogan "what would Jesus do?"
We don't know the answer, or better yet a clue.
Acknowledge him daily in everything by prayer,
He won't leave you ever, for he is always there.

He wants us to prosper and be in perfect health,
He'll supply our every need, and he'll also give us wealth.
All can't handle riches, for to some it is a sin,
Full of pride, arrogance and greed that consume you from within.

Seek ye first the kingdom, and all other things will come,
Your life will be much better when you let his will be done.
Our lives are not our own, we've been bought with a price
Salvation and redemption by accepting Jesus Christ.

SECTION V

AWESOME GOD
HEAVEN IS REAL
THE BEAUTY OF IT ALL
GOD'S GREAT TAPESTRY
THE MAN JESUS
WHAT'S YOUR STORY?
GET UP AND GO FORTH

AWESOME GOD

God, is like my shadow, that I see upon the ground
And though I can't see him, I know he's all around.
He watches over me and protects me from all harm,
For I am always safe, resting in his arms.

He's peace in- the- midst of chaos and trouble everywhere,
I will not be afraid because I know he's always there.
He's beside me in sorrow and comforts me in pain,
Without his love to sustain me I would go insane.

He wakes me in the morning, before the crack of dawn,
Ministers to my soul with instruction from the psalms.
The bible is a forecast of what you can expect,
If you can receive it, It's a compass to direct.

You cannot see the wind, but feel it in the air
I can talk to God, as I bow down, in prayer.
He's constantly molding me day by day,
For he is the potter, and I am the clay.

HEAVEN IS REAL

Heaven is for real, for this I know
But not because the bible tells us so.
I came to know Jesus at an early age,
Constantly reading the bible, page by page.

I called on his name as I knelt in prayer
Overcome by his spirit, he met me there
A light so bright, and a presence so strong,
I felt as if I was standing before his throne.

My tongue spoke a language that only he knew,
My heart felt the words that came pouring through
I couldn't control the utterance, or even the thought
But love and greatness was the feelings it brought.

My body felt light as a feather in the air,
I wanted to remain in that realm and stay there.
But that's just a touch of what lies in store
When I leave earth, to enter heaven's doors.

What an awesome moment, I shall never forget
It can't be compared to anything yet.
Heaven is real, for this I know,
When I leave this earth, that's where I'll go.

THE BEAUTY OF IT ALL

There are 7 wonders of the Ancient World, or so I have been told,
Like the Great Pyramid of Giza, and the Colossus of Rhodes.
The hanging Garden of Babylon, and all its awesomeness
Lighthouse of Alexandria and Temple of Artemis.

Mausoleum at Halicarnassus and the Statue of Zeus,
Are all sights of wonder to see and amuse.
I've never been to Paris or seen the Taj Mahal,
But God in all his splendor is behind the beauty of it all.

I've gone to the Bahamas on a cruise ship out at sea,
Jamaica and Grand Caymans and other ports of call
Traveled by plane to beautiful Hawaii are just
Memories to share the beauty of it all.

The most beautiful place I want to go, the streets are paved in gold,
Not in earthly tabernacles, but heavenly so I'm told.
So, when my life on earth is done, I'll answer to the call,
To spend eternity with my Lord, will be the beauty of it all.

GOD'S GREAT TAPESTRY

God has a tapestry, quite like no other
Full of great beauty and vibrant color
Forestry is green and thriving with life.
The parks in nature are a wonderful sight.

There's beauty in the clouds on a plane above,
The whitest of white, like a pretty, white dove.
Like bundles of cotton candy spread over the sky,
An awesome sight to see with the naked eye.

The beauty in the leaves that comes in the fall,
Like oranges, browns, reds yellows and all
Up in the mountains, from the highest peak
Glimpses of tapestry in the valley steep.

And the snowfall in winter, so quiet and sound
Of snowflakes and flurries hitting the ground.
And holidays of cheer, go hand in hand
With God's great tapestry covering the land.

No need to say more when spring arise
And all is fresh and new outside
The budding of flowers, and blossoming of leaves
Are all apart of God's great tapestry.

THE MAN JESUS

There is a man called Jesus, who walks upon the Earth
He came into this world, born of a virgin birth.
His purpose was to save humanity from their sins
And only through his blood, can our lives be cleansed.

Though narrow is the road, that leads to our salvation
And few that be, will find it with hope and revelation
Broad is the way of many, that will travel down that road
Facing trouble and destruction, unable to bear the load.

There is a man named Jesus, who guides us to this day,
And when you need to reach him, just close your eyes and pray.
He's never too busy to answer whenever you call,
He's omnipresent, omnipotent, and omniscient, for he is all.

WHAT'S YOUR STORY?

We all have a story, that only we can tell
Some bad, some good, others not so well
The things in life that we have seen,
Some fact, some fiction, or things we've dream.

Our stories are not always rosy and bright,
Some are of afflictions we endured over night
Others are the skeletons, that we've stored away
Some covered up and hidden to this very day.

Some stories are awesome, from the outside looking in
Though, dishonesty and cruelty will contemplate sin
There are stories of wealth from rags to riches,
Others through scams and crooked cyber glitches.

Some stories are revealing of how you made it out,
Despite all the odds and negative doubts.
You made great strides, now you are on the top,
A lavish to luxury living you can't even stop.

We all have a story, only we can tell
It may have started so rough but now its swell
My story is awesome, fulfilling and true,
I'm living for Jesus, what about you?

GET UP, GO FORTH

Get up and go forth, for God has need of you
You've been a little complacent in what you need to do.
Get out of your comfort zone, and ascribe to do much more
You'll never even imagine, what God has in store.

There are people you need to meet and places you need to go,
Your faith in God will lead you, and your blessing will overflow.
Get up and get moving, it's past time for a change
Don't be afraid to step out though it feels so oddly strange.

There's a blessing that awaits us when we make that vital step,
To reach a higher height and in God a deeper depth.
Get up and just get started, do what you need to do,
For the harvest is plentiful, but the laborers are few.